EASY-TO-READ FACTS OF RELIGIOUS HOLIDAYS CELEBRATED AROUND THE WORLD

Holiday Books for Children Children's Holiday Books

BABY PROFESSOR

EDUCATION KIDS

There are many religious holidays celebrated in the United States, as well as around the world. Read further to learn about more about these holidays, when they are celebrated, and how their traditions came about.

EASTER

This is a Christian holiday celebrating the resurrection of Jesus Christ from the dead. The Friday before Easter is known as Good Friday. This is known as the day that he was crucified at the cross.

This holiday moves around the calendar from year to year, but always occurs on Sunday. It lands on the first Sunday after the full moon which is after the vernal equinox.

The Sunday can occur anytime from March 22nd through April 25th. Christians around the world celebrate this holiday. It is known as one of the most

significant holidays that Christians celebrate. Many others celebrate it as an enjoyable holiday in spring.

In many countries, Orthodox Christians celebrate this holiday later than we do in the United States.

In Ethiopia, it is known as Fassika. Many kids will leave carrots out in case the Easter bunny is hungry.

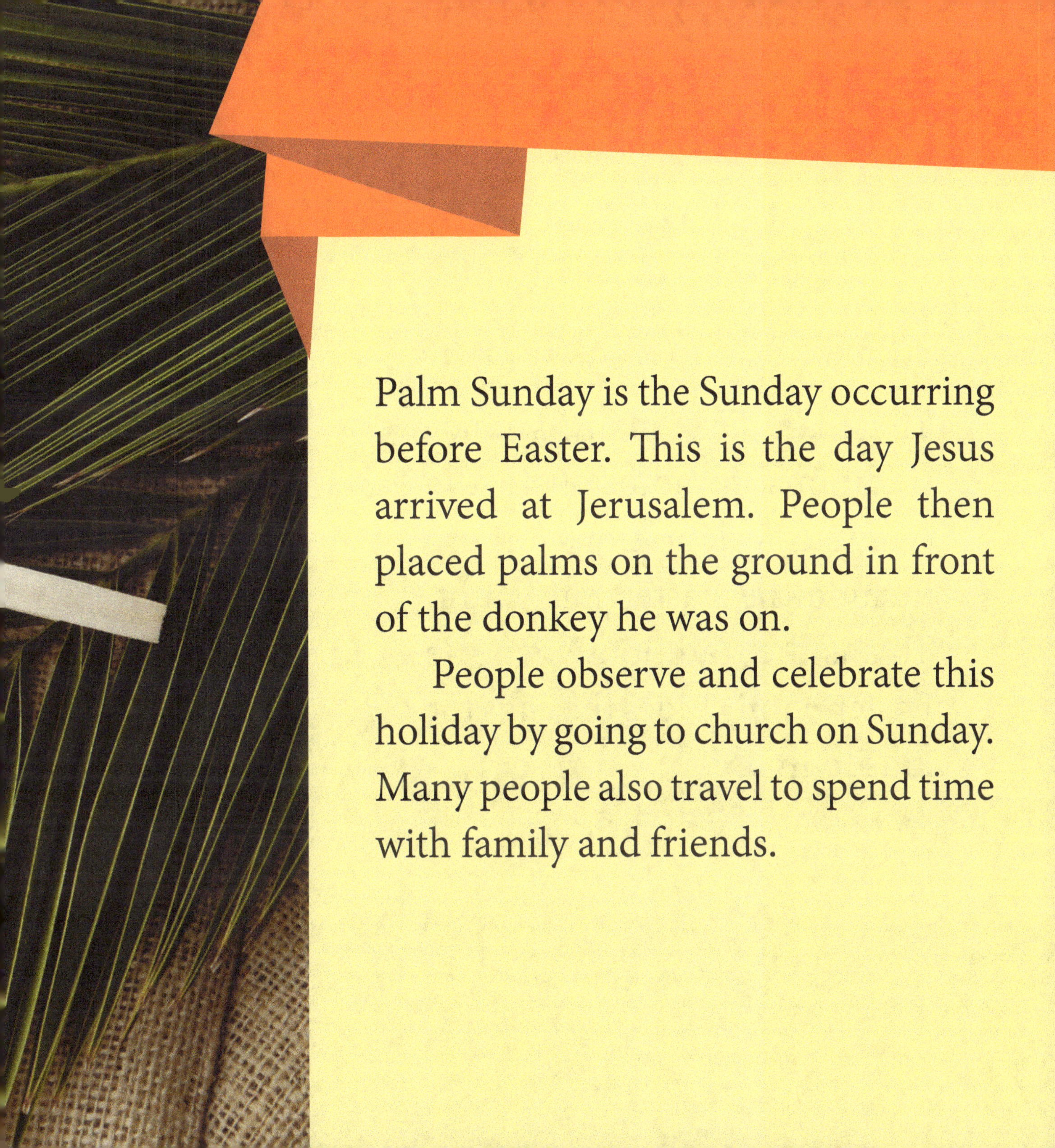

Palm Sunday is the Sunday occurring before Easter. This is the day Jesus arrived at Jerusalem. People then placed palms on the ground in front of the donkey he was on.

People observe and celebrate this holiday by going to church on Sunday. Many people also travel to spend time with family and friends.

There are also many secular traditions, in addition to the religious celebrations. These include the Easter Egg Hunt. This is the tradition when the Easter bunny hides the eggs for kids to find.

EASTER

Some additional traditions include the annual Easter Egg Roll presented at the White House. Easter baskets are filled with decorated hard boiled eggs, Easter bunnies made from chocolate, and Easter lilies. New York City puts on a great Easter parade every year.

Approximately 90 million chocolate Easter bunnies are made every year just for this holiday. The biggest Easter egg ever was more than 25 feet high!

ROSH HASHANAH

osh Hashanah is known as a religious holiday, celebrated by Jewish people. It commemorates the Jewish New Year in addition to the world's creation.

It typically lands during September, but it can be as late as October 5th. It is always celebrated 163 days after Passover but will never fall on a Wednesday, Friday or Sunday.

שיר השירים
191
שִׁיר הַשִּׁירִים
א שִׁיר הַשִּׁירִים אֲשֶׁר לִשְׁלֹמֹה: יִשָּׁקֵנִי מִנְּשִׁיקוֹת
פִּיהוּ כִּי־טוֹבִים דֹּדֶיךָ מִיָּיִן: לְרֵיחַ שְׁמָנֶיךָ טוֹבִים
שֶׁמֶן תּוּרַק שְׁמֶךָ עַל־כֵּן עֲלָמוֹת אֲהֵבוּךָ: מָשְׁכֵנִי
אַחֲרֶיךָ נָּרוּצָה הֱבִיאַנִי הַמֶּלֶךְ חֲדָרָיו נָגִילָה
וְנִשְׂמְחָה בָּךְ נַזְכִּירָה דֹדֶיךָ מִיַּיִן מֵישָׁרִים אֲהֵבוּךָ:
שְׁחוֹרָה אֲנִי וְנָאוָה בְּנוֹת יְרוּשָׁלַ͏ִם כְּאָהֳלֵי קֵדָר
שְׁלֹמֹה: אַל־תִּרְאוּנִי שֶׁאֲנִי שְׁחַרְחֹרֶת
בְּנֵי אִמִּי נִחֲרוּ־בִי שָׂמֻנִי נֹטֵרָה
שֶׁלִּי לֹא נָטָרְתִּי: הַגִּידָה לִּי

This holiday officially starts at nightfall. It occurs during Tishri. It is also known as Days of Awe or High Holy Days.

Jewish people that follow Judaism celebrate this day. To honor this holiday, Jewish people are not supposed to work.

This day is typically a time for prayer and spiritual reflection. A shofar is a horn which is blown to signify the beginning of a new year.

People will have family gatherings and send cards to celebrate this holiday. They prepare traditional foods which includes challah bread and sweets including honey and apples.

The foods will vary dependent on what part of the world they are located.

People will often meet one another saying "L'shanah tovah" which signifies "for a good year".

They also celebrate by performing a Tashikh, which is a ceremony where one's sins for the prior year can be "cast off" into water, like an ocean or river.

This ceremony will usually be performed when people walk into the body of water and then empty their pockets. In their pockets, they will usually carry small bits of bread.

YOM KIPPUR

Yom Kippur is also a Jewish holiday. It is also known as the "Day of Atonement" and is thought to be the holiest day for Jewish people.

When Egypt and Syria attacked Israel on Yom Kippur, this was the start of the Yom Kippur War. They hoped that the holiday might distract their army.

This holiday is celebrated ten days following Rosh Hashanah, at the ending of the High Holy Days. It generally takes place sometime between September and October.

Yom Kippur is celebrated by most of the Jewish community and is considered the holiest Jewish holiday.

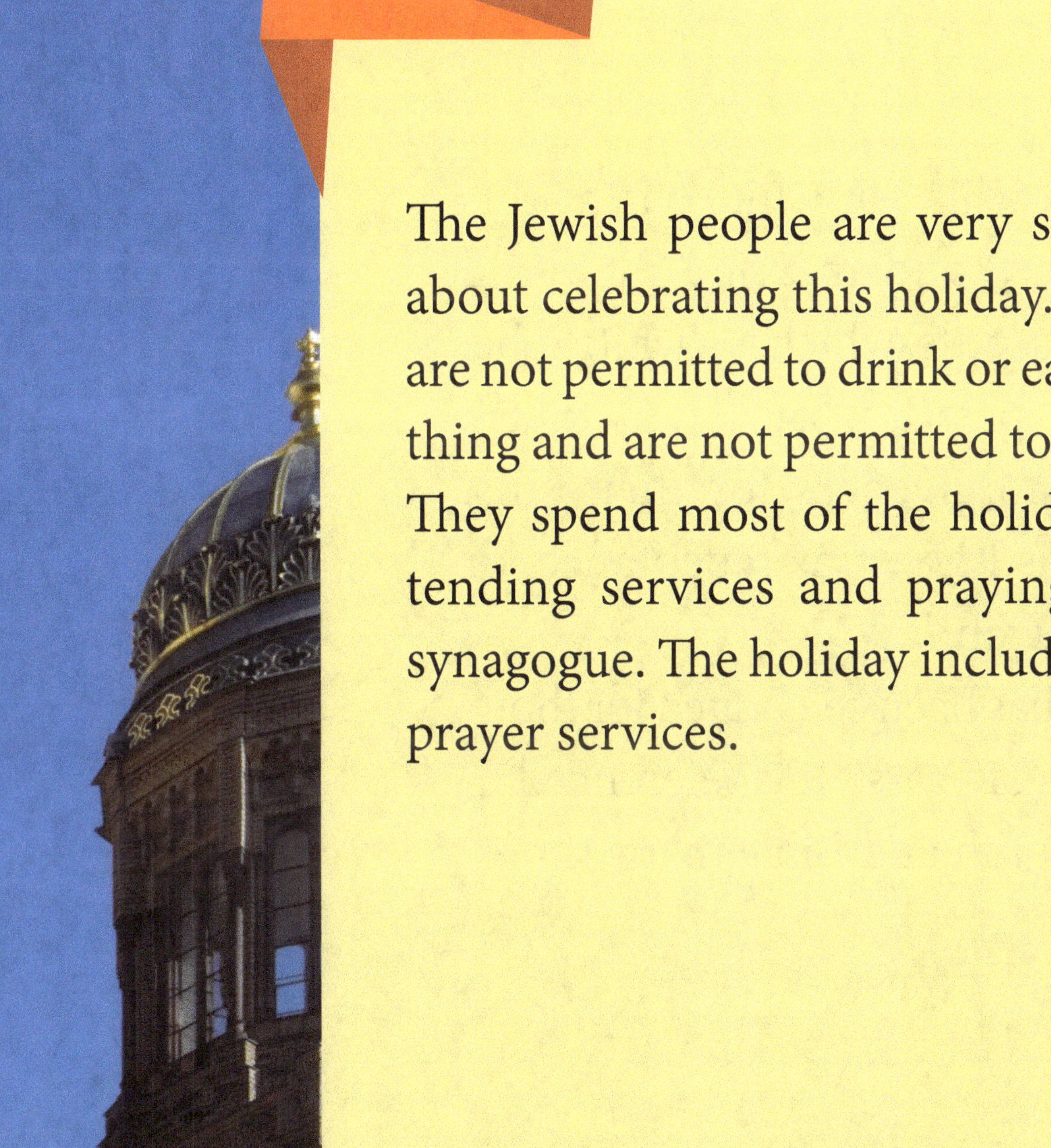

The Jewish people are very serious about celebrating this holiday. They are not permitted to drink or eat anything and are not permitted to work. They spend most of the holiday attending services and praying at a synagogue. The holiday includes five prayer services.

Many will wear white during this holiday, and married men will wear a kittle, which is a white robe. Their priority that day is to ask God forgiveness for their sins. This is known as repentance, or Teshuvah.

It has been celebrated for thousands of years. It is referenced in the Torah and Bible many times.

HAPPY
HANUKKAH

HANUKKAH

Hanukkah is celebrated by the Jewish Community and lasts for eight days and eight nights.

The word "Hanukkah" in Hebrew means "dedication." Hanukkah remembers the struggles dating back to 165 B.C.E., when the Jews overcame an attacking army and reclaimed the Temple in Jerusalem.

Legend states that the Jews discovered a lamp in the temple having barely enough oil to light the holy lamps for one night. Miraculously, it burned for eight nights. The Jews now celebrate Hanukkah by the lighting of a candle each night for eight nights. This candleholder is called a *Menorah*, representing the eight nights the lamp burned. Many celebrate this holiday by trading gifts each day. These candles should burn for 30 minutes after sunset.

Hanukkah was not considered as a major holiday until later in the 1800s. It is now one of the more popular Jewish holidays. It is also spelled Chanukkah and Chanukah.

They sing many hymns and songs which represent this special holiday. Maoz Tzur is sung every night and one of the candles are lit on the menorah.

Children will play with a *dreidel*, which is a top that has four sides. On the sides are letters that are of significance in the Hebrew religion.

Gelt (gold coins) are given to children. In the modern world, they are given chocolate wrapped in gold which makes them appear as gelt.

CHRISTMAS

Christians honor Jesus Christ's birth on Christmas. It is celebrated with gifts, stories, and prayer. One tradition relates to Santa Claus bringing gifts on Christmas Eve to children that have been good throughout the year. Each country celebrates with their own traditions.

Germans began the tradition of trimming the Christmas tree in the 16th century. They would bring the trees inside their houses and decorate them with nuts, candles, paper roses, and fruits.

Christmas is celebrated in many ways. Many will have family gatherings to exchange gifts and will go to church for services held Christmas Eve and Christmas Day.

This holiday celebrates the birth of Jesus Christ in Bethlehem. He was born to Mary and Joseph. In the New Testament, we learn that Jesus is God's Son and came to this Earth to die for our sins. Thirty-three years later, he was crucified. He was then buried in a tomb, but rose after three days and ascended to heaven.

While no one knows the exact day that he was born, it is believed that the Gospel of Luke pointed to Jesus' birth during December. It is also believed that the first celebrations occurred on January 6th and that December 25th was first referenced in a document dated 354 AD.

KWANZAA

KWANZAA

Kwanzaa is celebrated by African Americans in honor of their African roots and to intensify their bond with their traditional heritage. It centers around seven principles: unity, self-determination, collective responsibility, cooperative economics, purpose, creativity, and faith and will last seven days and seven nights, December 26 through January 1st.

They observe the days by lighting a candle each day which is meant to represent each principle. There are red, black, and green candles. One black candle which represents Unity. The three green candles stand for the future, and the three red candles represent their struggle with slavery.

There are many ceremonies held throughout the holiday. Many will decorate their home with African art and with the Kwanzaa colors of red, black, and green. They also wear traditional clothing. The women might wear a colorful wrap, known as a kaftan. The men might wear a dashiki, which is a colorful shirt, and a kufi, which is a hat.

On the final day of their celebration families will get together for a karamu, which is a feast. It may take place at a community center or local church.

Dr. Maulana Korenga created this holiday in 1966. The name is from Swahili and means "first fruits of the harvest". It was originally meant as a Christmas alternative, but then became an additional religious holiday similar to Christmas.

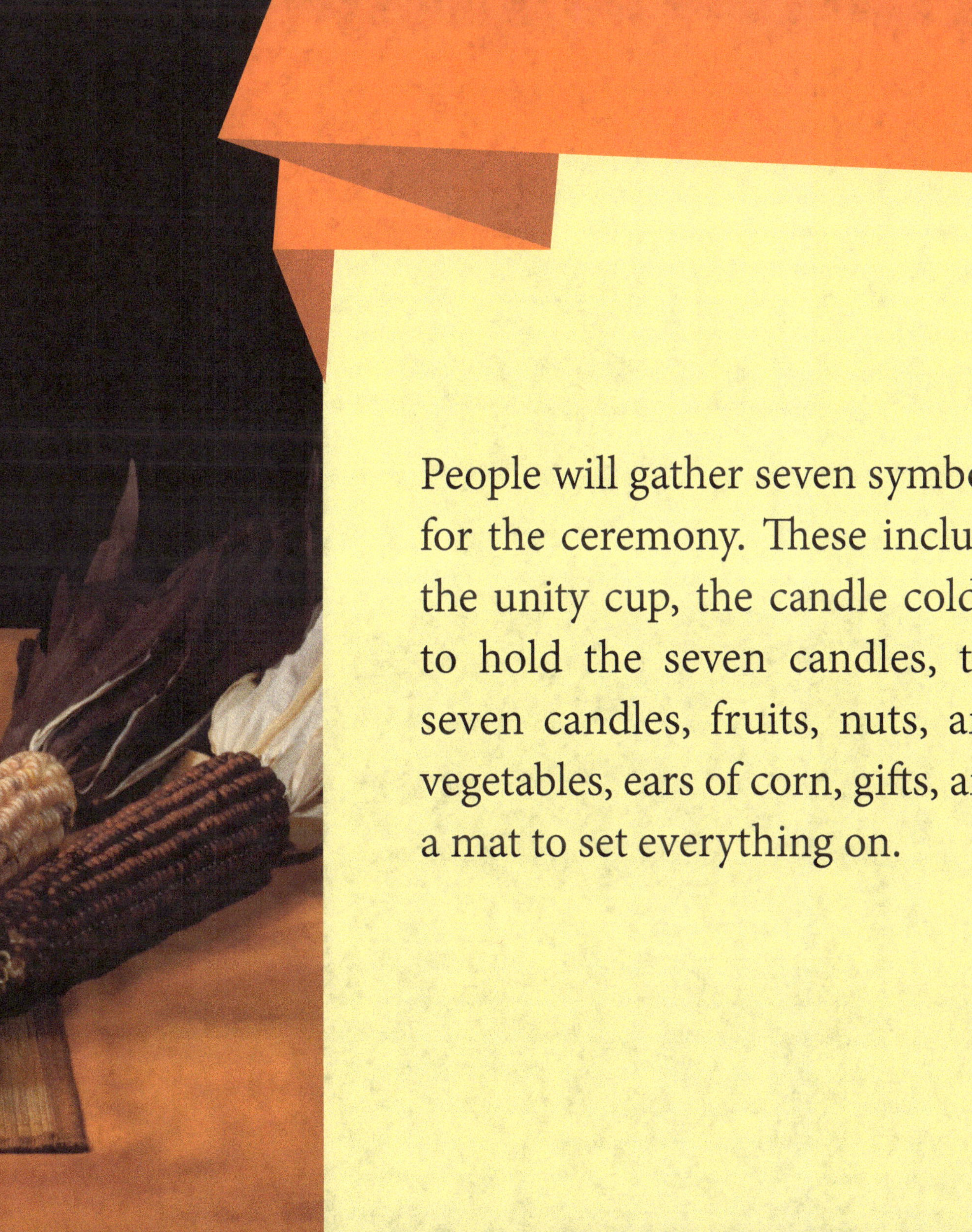

People will gather seven symbols for the ceremony. These include the unity cup, the candle colder to hold the seven candles, the seven candles, fruits, nuts, and vegetables, ears of corn, gifts, and a mat to set everything on.

Be sure to find out additional information on these holidays as well as others by researching the internet, going to your local library, and asking questions of your teachers, family, and friends.

Visit
BABY PROFESSOR
EDUCATION KIDS
www.BabyProfessorBooks.com
to download Free Baby Professor eBooks and view
our catalog of new and exciting Children's Books